YOUNG COMIC'S Guide

TO TELLING JOKES

BOOK 1

MICHAEL STRECKER

STERLING CHILDREN'S BOOKS

New York

To my wife, Jillian, and our sons,
Stephen and Joseph, with much love,
laughter, and gratitude.

STERLING CHILDREN'S BOOKS
New York

An Imprint of Sterling Publishing Co., Inc.
1166 Avenue of the Americas
New York, NY 10036

ISBN 978-1-4549-2130-1

Distributed in Canada by Sterling Publishing Co., Inc.
c/o Canadian Manda Group, 664 Annette Street
Toronto, Ontario, Canada M6S 2C8
Distributed in the United Kingdom by GMC Distribution Services
Castle Place, 166 High Street, Lewes, East Sussex, England BN7 1XU
Distributed in Australia by NewSouth Books
45 Beach Street, Coogee, NSW 2034, Australia

For information about custom editions, special sales, and premium
and corporate purchases, please contact Sterling Special Sales at 800-805-5489
or specialsales@sterlingpublishing.com.

Manufactured in Canada

Lot #:
2 4 6 8 10 9 7 5 3 1
11/16

www.sterlingpublishing.com

Design by Ryan Thomann

Contents

Introduction...................5

Tips for Telling Jokes
(No Joke) 6

So Funny, It's Scary 9

Animal Crackers 11

Laughing on the Job...... 19

These Jokes Won't Hurt
a Bit...........................28

Smiles for Miles............ 29

Jurassic Jokes................ 30

Sport Spoofs 31

Cutting Up with
Culture 35

Ships A-Joy 38

Funny Farm................... 39

Man, Oh, Man! 43

Stop in the Name of
Laugh! 47

Eye, That's Funny........... 49

Tree Hee-Hee 50

20,000 Laughs Under the
Sea 52

Holy Humor 55

LOL! 57

Fun and Names............. 65

Funny Business............. 68

The Ha-Ha House.......... 71

Doggone Funny 73

Funny Forecasts............ 74

Shockingly Funny 76

School Snickers 77

Ha! to the Chief............. 78

Literally Funny.............. 80

City Smirks................... 82

Mad, Mad World 84

Food for Fun 85

Love Laughs 91

Fairy Funny................... 92

Jokes That Don't Ring
a Bell 94

About the Author 96

INTRODUCTION

Have you ever dreamed of being a professional comedian? Imagine how cool it would be to make a roomful of people at a comedy club laugh or to host your own comedy television show. Or maybe you would just enjoy the thrill of knowing how to make your class or your family crack up.

Lots of people think the first thing you need to become a comic is a lot of jokes. Well, jokes are important, of course. But the first thing you need if you really want to be a great comedian is love. That's right, you have to love writing comedy, love thinking comedy, and, most important, love making people laugh.

If you do, then this is the book for you. This guide will help you learn how to tell a joke and inspire you to write your own jokes. It will give you some important dos and don'ts of comedy, too. And it will make you laugh.

To get your joke-telling, joke-writing, joke-loving pump primed, this guide also contains more than 600 original, hilarious jokes that will make you laugh 'til you cry, which is much nicer than crying 'til you laugh.

OK, ready to start your comedy career? Got your love? Let's go!

TIPS FOR TELLING JOKES
(NO JOKE)

1. *The rule of three:* Never tell more than three jokes in a row on the same subject. After the third joke about the same thing, people get tired. Tired people don't laugh much.

2. Know your audience. Not everyone will think every joke is funny. In fact, some people won't think anything is funny. These people usually end up in management.

3. Timing is very important. Don't tell your jokes too fast or too slowly.

4. To get your big break, give your audience a break. Don't tell too many jokes in a row. In fact, don't tell too many jokes anywhere.

5. If you know someone has a particular career or hobby, tailor the joke just for them. For instance, "How did the man like being a tailor?" "It suited him."

6. Act natural. Don't read your jokes out loud from this (or any) book. Memorize a couple and try to bring them up in conversation.

7. Even better than memorizing these jokes—try writing your own!

8. Don't read your jokes—but do read, read, read. The more words you know the more jokes you'll be able to understand and tell.

9. Often in comedy, what you don't say is as important as what you do say. Let your audience think for themselves. When you tell a joke, don't say the punch line too loudly or too obviously. Let the person you are telling the joke to figure it out. They will thank you with a big laugh.

10. Practice telling your jokes in front of a mirror—but don't crack it up.

Which type of monster eats the fastest?

A goblin

Where can you travel on a broom?

Every witch way

Why did Dracula lie down in the wrong coffin?

He made a grave mistake.

Did you get invited to Dracula's wedding?

Yes, it was an en*graved* invitation.

How did the doctor know Dracula was sick?

He kept coffin.

What did Dracula's parents tell him when he went to camp?

"Get to bed late and don't forget to fright."

What role did Dracula's son play on the baseball team?

Batboy

Who did the ghost bring to his family dinner?

His *ghoul*friend

What does a ghost say during a breakup?

"Can't we just be fiends?"

What is a baby ghost's favorite game?

Peekaboo!

How can you tell if a skeleton is upset?

He makes no bones about it.

How did Dracula's wife win the beauty contest?

The other vampires *paled* in comparison.

Where can you find information on monsters?

On *Wicked*pedia

How did the wizard's kid answer his father?

"Yes, seer!"

What did Frankenstein's monster do during a fight?

He bolted out of there.

What is the scariest part of a football field?

The *ghoul*posts

ANIMAL CRACKERS

How do turkeys eat?

They gobble, gobble.

Why was the chicken upset during the rainstorm?

He felt cooped up.

Why did everyone love the owl?

She was a real hoot.

When will the little snake arrive?

"I don't know, but he won't be long."

What is it like being a rabbit's parent?

It's a hare-raising experience.

Why should you not let a bear operate the remote?

He will keep pressing the *paws* button.

How does a skunk arrange its to-do list?

In odor of importance

What did the skunk philosopher say?

"I stink, therefore I am."

Why did the snake fail the spelling bee?

He couldn't think on his feet.

Where do lions live?

On Mane Street

What did the rabbit do when he ran out of cash?

He tried to burrow some money.

What do you call a large white bear who likes to take photos?

A Polaroid

Did you hear about the frog that parked in a no parking zone?

He got toad.

Why was the toy skunk broken?

It was out of odor.

What did the bird do when he saw the cat?

He tweeted for help.

What leader can't be trusted?

A lion king

Why did the lion cross the road?

To get to the other pride

Why did the chicken cross the road?

To get away from the lion

Why can't penguins fly?

There are no airports in Antarctica.

What does a rabbit need if it gets its fur wet?

A hare dryer

What do you call a pet rabbit handed down from one family member to the next?

An *hare*loom

What animal would frighten your aunt?

An *ant*eater

What do you call a rabbit that is always saying good-bye?

Wavy hare

Why don't dragons gain any weight?

They burn too many calories.

Why did the elephant think the countertop would hold him?

He took it for granite.

How did the crow get to Boston?

In a *caw*

What did the hungry whale do?

He yelled for kelp.

What doctor do fish go to?

The sturgeon general

Why did the cow jump over the moon?
    To get to the Milky Way

What is a pig's favorite breakfast?
    ***Oink*meal**

Why didn't the octopus write home?
    He ran out of ink.

What did the buck say when his wife asked him to paint the house?
    "Yes, deer."

What kind of seal tells you how wonderful you are?
    A seal of approval

What does a pig call his little toe?
    Pinky

How did the comic pig do at his first stand-up?
    He kept cracklin' everybody up.

Did you hear about the wolf's concert?
    It was a howling success.

HA
HA HA   HA
HA HA   HA
HA HA   HA
HA HA   HA
HA HA   HA
HA HA

How did the pig become a pastry chef?

He was good at bacon.

Why was the herder mad at the burglar?

He got his goat.

What did the polar bear leave the waitress?

The tip of the iceberg

Why do dogs like camping?

They love *ruffin'* it.

What is the one place where a dog will never shop?

A flea market

Who is the last bee to the hive?

The one that gets left *bee*hind

What kind of fish can keep the beat?

A drum

Why did the bird ask to be seated in a booth?

He didn't want to be a stool pigeon.

Where do elephants sit when they go to the movies?

In the peanut gallery

How does the zookeeper switch TV channels?

He uses a croc-o-*dial*.

What can you use to open a locked barn?

A don-*key*

What do you call a cat that steals someone's test answers?

A cheetah

Who is the most famous fish of them all?

A starfish

Why do giraffes make great friends?

They always stick their necks out.

What did the woman tell the man riding the Clydesdale?

"Get off your high horse!"

What do you call a pony that collects stamps, builds model trains, and knits?

A hobbyhorse

How do mice survive?

They *eke* out a living.

Why didn't the wild bird need a comb?

He was a bald eagle.

Where can you see eagles sing, dance, and tell jokes?

A talons show

What does a bird guarding her nest say when she hears something?

"Hawk! Who goes there?"

What do you call a seal leader?

A presidential seal

What did the giraffe say when he ate some oak trees?

"These are deciduous."

Why did the referee blow the whistle when the chicken was off sides?

It was a fowl.

Why did Mickey Mouse wear a hat and sunglasses when he went shopping?

He wanted to avoid the papaRATzzi.

Why can't Charley sing?

Charley's hoarse.

What kind of pig is always the first to volunteer?
   A guinea pig

Where did the small, furry astronaut want to go?
   To otter space

Why did the mosquito ask for a red crayon?
   He wanted to draw blood.

What did the confused insect say?
   "To bee or not to bee . . ."

What book did the famous owl research appear in?
   In "Who's Who"

LAUGHING ON THE JOB

Why did the man try to sell an old deck of cards?
   He was a used card salesman.

Why did the man get fired from his job at the coin factory?
   He stopped making cents.

Why did the honey maker never stop?

She was as busy as a bee.

What does an angry doctor give you?

A cross examination

Why did the taxi driver get fired?

He drove everyone to tears.

What did the patriotic optometrist ask his patients?

"O say can you see?"

What is the goal of a grammar teacher?

Not to write any wrongs

Why didn't anyone like the director?

He was always making a scene.

How did the contortionist's job interview go?

He put his foot in his mouth.

How did the woman become a contortionist?

It was a stretch.

How did the referee's job interview go?

He blew it.

Why did the bell ringer not have to use his hands?
His ears were ringing.

Why did the chef yell at the food to cook faster?
He was a pressure cooker.

Why did the stuntwoman quit?
She kept running into brick walls.

Why did the cemetery close?
Business died off.

Why did the old businessman buy four wheels?
He wanted to retire.

What kind of music do geologists like?
Hard rock

Why did the coroner quit?
It was a dead-end job.

Why was the trash collector upset?
He got canned.

Where did the trumpet player go on vacation?
Cape Horn

Why was everyone annoyed at the trumpet player?

She kept tooting her own horn.

Why didn't the impatient person get hired by the restaurant?

She couldn't wait.

Why did the man's head get big?

He had a swell idea.

What instrument does Phil play?

Phil's harmonica

Why did the baker get fired?

She kept loafing around.

What did the robber say when he held up the bakery?

"Hand over the dough. I don't want no truffle!"

What did the new broom factory owner do?

She made sweeping changes.

How did the broom factory manager propose?

He swept his fiancée off her feet.

Why did the exterminator lose his job?
  He wouldn't hurt a fly.

Why did the welder retire?
  She got burned out.

Why did the traffic cop ask for a tissue?
  To clear the congestion

Why did the comedian become a chiropractor?
  She liked to pull people's legs.

Why did the tailor choose his profession?
  It suited him.

What's it like being a boxer?
  Beats me.

What is it like working in a cheese factory?
  It's grate!

Why did the veterinarian go to the optometrist?
  She kept seeing Spots before her eyes.

Why didn't the manager need a forklift?
  He realized the fork wasn't that heavy.

Why is it so hard to leave the Velcro factory?
You become attached.

How did the glue factory employee feel?
Stuck

What did the submarine engineers demand?
A raise

How is the horse business?
Stable

How is the sprinkler business?
Drying up

Why did everyone have fun at the service station?
It was a gas.

How is the news business?
Good and bad

When is no news not good news?
When you're a reporter

What's the best thing about working at a coffeehouse?
The perks

How is the gambling business?

It's a good bet.

What is a hairstylist's favorite Olympic sport?

Curling

What is the best way to earn milk money?

Work at a dairy farm

What is the best way to learn how to be a bricklayer?

Trowel and error

What is the dentist's favorite game?

Tooth or Dare

How does a dentist advertise?

Word of mouth

What did the angry electrician do?

He blew a fuse.

What job pays you to whistle while you work?

A referee

Why would Pinocchio be a good reporter?

He is so nosy.

Did you hear about the woman who opened three bakeries in three weeks?

She was really on a roll.

Where do pilots get their hair cut?

At the *hair*port

Why did no one trust the artist?

He was sketchy.

How did the mortician do on the first day of his job?

He knocked 'em dead.

Why was the snail a good worker?

She always arrived on slime.

What singer could have worked at a dry cleaner?

Elvis *Press*-ley

Why did the woman get a job at the coin factory?

She wanted change.

Why did the meeting with the painter not go well?

"He brushed me off."

Why can't you lie to a radiologist?

He'll see right through you.

What do you call a doctor who is always joking?

An aller*jest*

Why did Alexander Graham Bell invent the telephone?

It was his calling.

What do you call twenty uninterested people sitting around a table?

A bored room

How did you open a fried chicken restaurant with no experience?

You wing it.

Why did the astronaut's trip to Mars go badly?

He didn't planet very well.

HA HA HA HA HA HA HA HA HA

THESE JOKES WON'T HURT A BIT

Why didn't the dental hygienist like her award?

It was a plaque.

What is the best thing to use to fix a broken tooth?

Toothpaste

Why did the dentist like the brush?

It was a fine-tooth comb.

Was the test to get into dental school hard?

No, it was tooth or false.

Why did the road say "ouch"?
There was a fork in it.

Why was the road nervous?
It was about to get graded.

How did the artist cross the river?
On a drawbridge

What did the taxi driver say when the tourist gave her a bad tip?
"It's not fare!"

How does a car let you know it is joking?
It gives a hoodwink.

What is the best companion for a road trip?
A car*pet*

What do you call twelve gas stations is a row?
A bunch of fuels

JURASSIC JOKES

What does a dinosaur do when he is lost?
Look at the *Mapusaurus*

What do you get when you ride a Stegosaurus all day?
A dino*sore*

Why did the dinosaur refuse to wear deodorant?
He didn't want to be ex-*stink.*

What do you call a groovy dinosaur?
Dino-mite

What is a caveman's favorite food?
A club sandwich

SPORT SPOOFS

Why was the weightlifter upset?
She worked with dumbbells.

What do lightning and a good batter have in common?
They don't strike often.

How did the man feel after he bench-pressed
300 pounds?
**Like a great weight had been lifted off
his chest**

What did they call Shakespeare when he lifted
200 pounds?
A strong Will

What happened when the quarterback ran off with
the clock?
Time ran out.

Why did the ex-football player make a good leader?
He tackled problems head-on.

What kind of match is hard to get out of the box?
A wrestling match

Why did none of the baseball players have
black eyes?
No one batted an eye.

Why was the Cyclops a good athlete?
He always kept his eye on the ball.

What did the golf pro tell his student?
"Just go *fore* it."

Why did the coach drive a bulldozer to the game?
He wanted to level the playing field.

Why didn't the dessert hit the ball far?
It was a Bundt cake.

How did the soccer player pay for dinner?
By footing the bill.

When the clothes had a race, who won?

It was a tie.

What kind of race do pants have?

A clothes one

What do you sound like if you keep repeating that you ran a three-minute mile?

Like a broken record

What kind of weights do you start with?

Paperweights

Why didn't the batter answer his phone?

He was out.

Why did the fisherman continue to fish?

Because he was hooked

Why are colds good at fishing?

They're always catching.

How did the genius stay in shape?

Graduation exercises

Why didn't the man want to go bow hunting?

The very thought made him quiver.

Why was the man afraid to go hunting?

He had mousse in his hair.

Why did the runner put glue on the bottom of her shoes?

Because she thought her coach told her to paste herself.

What happened when the witches played the wizards in baseball?

The witches swept them.

What do a symphony conductor and sports announcer have in common?

They both need to know the score.

Would a tennis match between two brains go well?

If memory serves

Why did the quarterback buy a bandage?

The coach told him he was going to cut him.

What was Lady Gaga called as a baby?
Lady Goo-Goo

Who is a very chivalrous actress?
Keira Knightley

What planet are Superman, Batman, and Wonder Woman from?
The Planet of the Capes

What is Sylvester Stallone's favorite mountain range?
The Rockies

What kind of books does orange juice read?
Pulp fiction

Why was Han Solo worried about attacking the Death Star?

He thought he might have bitten off more than he could Chewie.

Why did the bar of Irish Spring get the lead part in a TV show?

It was a soap opera.

What do you call a stage production by ponies?

Horseplay

Why couldn't the woman afford the flower painting?

She ran out of Monet.

Why was the book about grapes so popular?

It had lots of juicy details.

What do you call a group of flies trapped in a home?

Desperate houseflies

What did King Tut's mommy say to him when he was upset?

"Tut, Tut, don't cry."

What kind of shampoo do the presidents on Mt. Rushmore use?

Head & Shoulders

What would happen if there were an earthquake at Mt. Rushmore?

Heads would roll

What happened when the completion of Mt. Rushmore was delayed?

The whole country became headwaiters.

Why should Charlie Brown be on Mt. Rushmore?

Because he's a blockhead.

What was the hardest part of making Mt. Rushmore?

Staying ahead of the competition

How did the Mt. Rushmore supervisor motivate the sculptor?

"Rush more."

What can you see at Mt. Rushmore?

Heads of state

SHIPS A-JOY

What is the smartest kind of boat?
A scholarship

What is the cheapest boat you can buy?
A sale boat

What do you call a citrus fruit on a submarine?
Sublime

What kind of lettuce is never served on ships?
Iceberg

How did the land know the ship would find it?
It was shore.

Why wouldn't the captain let the heavy metal band on board?
He didn't want to rock the boat.

Where are the diaper-changing stations located on a ship?
On the poop deck

Where is detention located on a ship?

The stern

Where do dogs play on a ship?

The bow-wow

Why did the sea captain refuse to get a new hat?

He didn't want to get capsized.

Where do cotton swabs go?

Down the *Earie* Canal

What is the Q-tip's job on the ship?

Swabbing the deck

FUNNY FARM

Why wasn't the woman upset when she lost her ring while planting vegetables?

She knew it would *turnip.*

Why was the bull afraid to leave the barn?

He was a *coward*.

What gave the sack of grain a cold?

A wheat germ

Why did the squash win the beauty pageant?

It was *gourd*-geous.

What do you call a gourd's relative?

A pump-kin

What happened when the cucumber fell into the barrel of vinegar?

It got itself into a pickle.

How do you grow cantaloupes?

Water melons.

What kind of fruit loves the sea?

Naval oranges

What beans love the water?

Navy beans

What kind of melon will never run off and get married?

A *can't elope*

How did the rancher know she had too many cattle?

She over*herd* it.

What did the cowboy say when the cow shouted at him?

"I herd you!"

What do you call a rich steer?

A cash cow

What do you call a cow that is always asking for money?

A *mooch*

What do you do if your cash cow runs out of money?

Try your piggy bank.

What does a cow give her baby?

S*mooches*

How did the woman with the baby cow injure herself?

She pulled her calf.

Why was the jack-o'-lantern scared to go to the big city?

It was a country pumpkin.

What did the farmer want from the robber?

His feed back

How does a Spanish cow say "thank you"?

"*Moo*-chas *gracias*"

What are the most musical bugs?

The Beetles

Why did the horse lose the election?

Too many *neigh* votes

What do you say if someone lines your flower bed with pine straw?

"Thank you very mulch."

What do they grow on a car farm?

Bumper crops

What kind of vegetables grow on shirts?

***Collar*d greens**

MAN, OH, MAN!

Why did the man take the chair out of the doctor's office?
> **The nurse told him to take a seat.**

Why did the woman swallow a key?
> **She had lockjaw.**

Why was the runner carrying a net?
> **He was trying to catch his breath.**

Why did the woman bring a baseball glove to work?
> **She was trying to catch up.**

Why did the man bring a fishing pole to work?
> **He planned to play hooky.**

Why did the woman get fired at the pants factory?
> **She was a real slacker.**

Why did the man buy a new computer every day?
Because his mom told him, "An Apple a day keeps the doctor away."

Why did the politician wear sneakers?
She was running for office.

Why did the man put his head on the piano keys?
He wanted to play by ear.

Why did the singer place the microphone against her chest?
She knew the song by heart.

What did the man fear most from the male sheep?
The ramifications

Why did the man think his wife was a carpenter?
She told him she made the bed.

Why did the woman think her husband was joking?
He told her *he* made the bed.

What did the man say to his friend who created a best-selling lotion?
"Don't rub it in."

What did the woman say when she won the coin toss?

Thanks for the heads up.

Why didn't the man want the operation?

He knew it would cost him an arm and a leg.

How do you know if a mailman is angry?

He stamps out of the room.

Why did the woman bring a pen and paper to the duel?

She wanted to be ready to draw.

Why did the scientist move to the Arctic?

She realized her fate was seals.

What should you do if Mr. Smith tries to escape?

Lock Smith.

What should the jailer do if Ms. Ness tries to escape?

Loch Ness.

Why didn't the man from the North Pole like the man from the South Pole?

They were polar opposites.

What do comics and computers hate the most?

Hacks

Did you hear about the video of the man sneezing?

It went viral.

Why didn't the man buy the hat?

It fit like a glove.

Why did the man lie after lunchtime?

He was full of baloney.

What did the woman say after she had been playing classical piano for three hours?

"My Bach hurts."

What is a woman next to you on a train?

A near Miss

Why did the man close down his scuba shop?

He was in way over his head.

HA HA HA HA HA HA HA HA HA

What did the policeman tell the mime?
"**You have the right to remain silent.**"

What kind of day is it when you've gotten a ticket?
One fine day

Why did the detective want to know who chopped down the tree?
He was stumped.

Why did the thief lie down and take a nap?
The police officer told him he was under a rest.

What did the cop say when she caught the statue thief?
"**This is a bust.**"

Why didn't the woman want to work at a branch bank?
She was afraid of a stick-up.

Was the bank robber armed?
Yes, and he had legs, too.

Why did the art thief plead innocent?

He was framed.

Did you hear about the woman who tried to rob a bank with a banana?

She got off on a peel.

Why didn't the mobsters want to talk in the cornfield?

The place had too many ears.

Why can't you hide in a potato patch?

The place has too many eyes.

Did you hear about the man who tried to rob a bank with a pig?

It squealed.

Did you hear about the woman who robbed the bakery?

She took the cake.

What did the kidnapper do when he wanted to lose weight?

He *ransom.*

What happened when the gym owner was robbed?

She lost a lot of weight.

Why didn't the gym's alarm go off?
It was a dumbbell.

Why did the guy break into the gym?
He couldn't *weight* for it to open.

What did the police say when they heard about the
ten dead chickens?
They suspected fowl play.

EYE, THAT'S FUNNY

What do you need to read a computer in
the dark?
Night Googles.

What do you do if you have your eyes on a car?
***Go to the doctor!* Your eyes shouldn't be
on a car!**

Why did the boy need special glasses to read
his grades?
He got a 3-D report card.

What kind of phone might need glasses?

An eye-Phone

What is it called when two eyes apologize to each another?

Eye make up

What do eyes and schools have in common?

Pupils

What is a pea's favorite mobile device?

An iPod

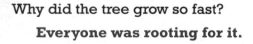

TREE HEE-HEE

What happened when the tree saw the man with an ax?

It became as stiff as a board.

Why did the tree grow so fast?

Everyone was rooting for it.

What is the best way to cut down a tree?

Call it a shrub.

What do you use to give a tree a shot?

A pine needle

How does a squirrel like his ice cream?

In a pinecone

Why was the oak tree upset?

The pine tree kept needling him.

What kind of illustrations does a tree make?

Stick figures

What does a tree do when it's angry?

It packs its trunk and leaves.

Did you know there is a man-eating tree?

"Yes, and I heard its bark is even worse than its bite."

What does a tree say to its foliage every fall?

"I can't believe you're leaving me."

What do you call a coconut tree that loves books?

A palm reader

What do trees and dogs have in common?

Bark

What did the tree do at night?

Slept like a log.

20,000 LAUGHS UNDER THE SEA

Why did the jellyfish do poorly in school?

He was a no-brainer.

How does a fisherman make money?

Net income

What can a fish never do?

Travel _overseas_

How did the fish lose so much weight?

He was on a liquid diet.

What does a baby whale do when he is upset?

Blubber

How does a fisherman train for football practice?
He opens his tackle box.

What do you call a fish who only thinks of himself?
Sel-fish

What was the sea creature strike called?
Octopi Wall Street

How did the octopus welcome the scuba diver?
With open arms

How did the scuba diver respond when the octopus grabbed him?
With a sucker punch

What is a knight's favorite type of seafood?
Swordfish

Why did the baked trout arrive after dessert?
It was a fish out of order.

Why are hammerhead sharks fair?
They can see both sides.

HA HA HA   HA HA HA   HA HA HA   HA HA HA   HA HA HA   HA HA HA

What is the saddest sea creature?

A blue whale

Why wouldn't the mermaid marry the whale?

She couldn't get over the hump.

Why didn't anyone like the Great Lake?

She thought she was Superior.

How did the whale look in a tuxedo?

Killer

Where do fish go when they are sick?

To the nurse shark

What do you call a frightened sailor?

Chicken of the sea

Why did the frog have a pole and tackle box?

He was going fly-fishing.

Where can you go to buy shrimp?

A prawn shop

What did the fish guard say?

"Who goes there, fin or anemone?"

HOLY HUMOR

What is the Pope's favorite scent?

Potpourri

Why did the rabbi like to drive people around?

He wanted to be a *shofar*.

What did people say when the skunk entered the church?

"Pew."

Why did the minister think the woman had lost her faith?

She said his sermon was unbelievable.

Why did Noah and his wife get along so well?

They were two of a kind.

How was Jonah's boat trip?

He had a whale of a time.

What is Jonah's favorite band?

Bob Marley and the Whalers

Why was it raining pennies from heaven?
Climate change

What do you call a group of rabbis on roller skates?
Holy rollers

How did the dentist pay for his vision exam?
An eye for a tooth

Did you hear about the priest with the great sense of humor?
He entertained the Masses.

What do you call a group of horseback riders racing to church?
A steeplechase

What kind of animals go to church?
Birds of prey and angelfish

What kind of animal chants the service?
Chipmonks

Why didn't anyone like the Swiss cheese?
He was holier than thou.

LOL!

Why was the precious metal so silly?
    It was fool's gold.

What is a thirteen-year-old grain of salt?
    A salt-*teen*

Why was the king good at measuring things?
    He was a ruler.

How does the postmaster give his permission?
    With a stamp of approval

Did you hear about the rude clock?
    It wouldn't give anyone the time of day.

What finger do you use to make a phone call?
    Your ring finger

Why were the Easter eggs nervous?

It was time to dye.

What do birds love to do on social media?

Tweet, tweet!

What did the cactus wear to the formal?

A cac-tie

How did the first person realize that the sun rises in the east?

It just dawned on him.

What do you call a tiny, tiny, tiny bottle of mouthwash?

A micro-Scope

What vowels live on a farm?

E, I, E, I, O

How do the cells in your body communicate?

Cell phones

Who invented the ballpoint pen?

The Incas

What test is easy for a dad?

A pop quiz

What do you call a seat at a boring lecture?

A yawn chair

What do a Laundromat and a casino have in common?

They are both places where you can lose your shirt.

How did the sock win the race?

It started out on the right foot.

Why did the man keep pressing the button of his shirt?

It was permanent press.

What do you call talking on the phone with the person next to you?

A close call

Why was the army in debt?

It charged a lot.

What do you do at a math party?

Eat pi and square dance.

Why is investing in coal relaxing?
It gives you piece of mine.

What is one thing you don't want to buy with no strings attached?
A kite

How did the pasta win the academic bowl?
He used his noodle.

What do you call a knight who does not show up on time?
Late knight

Where is the safest place to keep poles?
In a pole vault

Did you hear about the girl who couldn't stop Tweeting?
She was all a-Twitter.

What did the red vegetable wear to the rodeo?
"Beets me."

What Italian explorer loved to carry a wooden mallet?
Marco Polo

What kinds of dinosaurs love hip-hop music?

Raptors

What the worst thing about an earache?

It's *ear*-itating.

How did the egg become a star?

She got a big break.

Why are fishermen good at geometry?

They like to angle.

What did the prisoner say when the executioner couldn't tie a knot?

"No noose is good noose."

Why was the apartment owner so suspicious?

He had a complex.

Who is your coolest relative?

Aunt Arctica

What do you call a watch that is stuck in ice?

Frozen in time

HA HA HA   HA HA HA   HA HA HA   HA HA HA   HA HA HA   HA HA HA   HA HA HA

What's one thing you won't find in a china shop?

A break room

What is another term for shoe shopping?

Sole searching

Why did the cell phone do so well in school?

It was a smartphone.

Did you hear about the sailor who couldn't finish the alphabet?

He got lost at C.

Why wouldn't the grape dry in the sun?

It was *unraisinable*.

If you drop an apple and an orange from the top of a building, which will hit the ground first?

You can't compare apples and oranges.

Why are rock stars so cool?

They have a lot of fans.

Why did the woman keep trying on different wigs?

She liked to put on hairs.

What is the rudest part of a computer?

The cursor

What does a hurt lemon need?

Lemon aid

What is the best advice you were ever given?

"A cannibal will only have you over for dinner once."

What kind of model works at car shows?

A model T

Why didn't anyone like the movie about the unsharpened pencil?

It was pointless.

What did the professor call the element that suddenly appeared on her periodic table?

The element of surprise

What do you call organs lined up in a perfectly straight row?

Organization

HA
HA HA HA HA HA HA HA

Why did the man give away a thousand pianos?

He was an organ donor.

What kind of shoes can talk?

Converse

Why do some people insist on handwritten notes instead of email?

They like to push the envelope.

What do you call an escalator being transported by airplane?

A flight of stairs

What happened after the moon ate a big meal?

It was full.

What do you call someone who spends all his money on a fortune-teller?

A seersucker

What did the window feel when it broke?

It was a pane-ful experience.

HA HA HA

FUN AND NAMES

HELLO
my name is

What is the name of the trapeze artist?
Annette

What is the name of the wealthy man?
Rich

What is the name of the best lawyer?
Sue

What is the name of the famous meteorologist?
Gail

Who is the head of the IRS?
Bill

What is the name of the head pharmacist?
Phil

What is the name of the Pulitzer Prize winner?
Arthur

What is the name of the famous archaeologist?
Doug

What is the name of the valet?
Parker

Who thinks it's all about "me, me?"
Mimi

Who missed the bus?
Walker

Who gives it his all?
Max

Who won the gold medal in discus throwing?
Chuck

Who is the hardest-working person in the company?
Ernest

What is the name of the new painter?
Art

Who is the new PE teacher?
Jim

Who can really get into a good book?
Paige

What is the name of the sculptor?
Chip

Who do you go to for an honest opinion?
Frank

Who do you call when you need to redo your kitchen floor?
Tyler

Who loves to go to a casino?
Betty

What is the name of the trumpet player?
Blair

Who is the new
announcer?
Mike

Who should you go
hiking with?
Hillary

Who should you call to
fix your phone?
Belle

Who's the happiest girl?
Joy

Who is an early riser?
Dawn

Who do you call
when you need some
illustrations?
Drew

Who likes to go
fishing?
Rod

What was the name
of the man caught
stealing?
Rob

What do you call a girl
who loves the beach?
Sandy

What do you call a
very bright kid?
Sonny

What is a name that
gets passed down
every generation?
Gene

Who has a lot of
chickens?
Cooper

Who cries a lot?
Waylon

FUNNY BUSINESS

What is the hardest part of getting hired at a shoe store?

Getting your foot in the door

How is the sock repair business?

Darn good

How is the electricity business?

Shocking!

How is the movie business?

Reeling

How is the tanning business?

Fading

How is the airplane business?

Soaring

How is the tennis business?
Good net income

How is the ice business?
Cool

How is the pool business?
Treading water

How is the boat business?
Staying afloat

How is business at a surf shop?
It comes in waves.

Why didn't the woman become a neurologist?
She lost her nerve.

Why couldn't the woman fix the toy gun?
It was shot.

Why did the man quit being a palm reader?
He didn't see a future in it.

How good was the man at palm reading?
He was the best, hands down.

What do you call a comedy club filled with allergy sufferers?

Ha-Ha-Choo.

What do you call the publicist for a bike shop?

The head *spokes*person

How did the baker become rich?

He made a lot of dough.

Why didn't the man become a negotiator?

He talked himself out of it.

Why did the man quit his job working on the bridge?

It really took a toll on him.

What do you call a pushy salesman?

Why would you want to call a pushy salesman?

Why do bakers make good actors?

They know lots of rolls.

Why did the doctor lose her temper?

She ran out of patients.

Why would the waiter be a good detective?
   He's good at getting tips.

Why did the woman fail the acupuncture test?
   She didn't get enough points.

Why did the masseuse get fired?
   She rubbed her customers the wrong way.

Why didn't the relationship with the trash collector work out?
   He dumps everyone.

How did the elevator operator feel about getting fired?
   It floored him.

Where is the best city to open a comedy club?
   Baja, California

THE HA-HA HOUSE

Why was the ceiling sad?
It only had one fan.

Why was the floor sad?

People walked all over it.

Why was the chair sad?

All it did was sit around all day.

Why was the sink sad?

It felt drained.

Why was the dishwasher sad?

Sometimes it felt empty.

Why was the closet sad?

It had a lot of hang-ups.

Why was the refrigerator happy?

It kept its cool.

What did Hayley use to clean the kitchen sink?

Hayley's Comet

Why wouldn't the insect go inside the house?

He didn't want to bug anyone.

What do you call a person who loves ceilings?

A ceiling fan

Why didn't the arm want to buy the house?

The place had no elbow room.

Why are termites bad guests?

They eat you out of house and home.

DOGGONE FUNNY

How did the dog get the tick to leave him alone?

He made a flea bargain.

What do you call a dog in the desert?

A hot dog

What do you call a dog at the North Pole?

A chili dog

What is the most important part of a dog's diet?

_Ruff_age

Did you hear about the beagle who forgot his wife's birthday?

He's in the doghouse.

What do you call a sheep herder from Munich?

A German shepherd

Why was the dog busy on Father's Day?

It had four paws.

FUNNY FORECASTS

Why did the cloud make noise during the storm?

Because when it rained, it snored.

What's the forecast for Halloween?

Cloudy and ghoul

What is the weather supposed to be on New Year's Eve?

Party cloudy

What's the weather supposed to be on Christmas?

It's calling for rain, dear.

Why didn't the meteorologist show up for work?
She was under the weather.

What do storm clouds and kings have in common?
They both *reign*.

Why did everyone like the breeze?
It was cool.

Why did the rain want to lose weight?
It was heavy.

Why were the showers disorganized?
They were scattered.

When did the showers get organized?
During the gathering storm

HA HA HA HA HA HA HA HA HA HA HA HA HA HA HA HA HA HA HA HA HA HA HA HA

Why did the fog fail the test?
    It was dense.

Why did the sun pass the test?
    It was bright.

Why couldn't the snow pay attention in class?
    It drifted.

SHOCKINGLY FUNNY

What's a good way to greet an electrician?
    "Watt's up?"

What's the best way to pay an electrician?
    Wire her the money.

What kind of car does an electrician drive?
    A Volts-wagon

Why did the electrician read fashion magazines?
    He wanted to stay current.

What do you call a math class with only three kids?

Odd

What do you call it if three kids join it?

Even

Does learning how to subtract help children?

It makes all the difference.

"My twin brother and I are in the same statistics class together."

"What is the chance of that?"

What happened when the boy couldn't solve the addition problem?

He was nonplussed.

What is the first thing the math teacher did when she bought her house?

She made an addition.

How many math problems could the student solve?
   Sum

Why did the lumberjack get bad grades?
   He was always cutting up in class.

What did the teacher say when the boy said he
wanted to go to Pluto?
   "Don't be Goofy."

HA! TO THE CHIEF

Which U.S. president cleaned his own dishes?
   Washington

Which U.S. president could work in a sausage
factory?
   Lincoln

Which U.S. president's family is creepy and kooky,
mysterious and spooky?
   The Adams family

Which U.S. president would make a good cartoon character?

Garfield

Which U.S. president probably would have liked *Sesame Street*?

Grover Cleveland

Which U.S. president loved air conditioning?

Coolidge

Which U.S. president vacuumed a lot?

Hoover

Which U.S. president could easily cross a river?

Ford

Which U.S. presidents did their own landscaping?

The Bushes

Which U.S. president did not see well?

Hayes

HA HA HA HA HA HA HA HA HA HA HA HA HA HA HA HA HA HA

LITERALLY FUNNY

What do you call a street where Shakespeare, Edgar Allen Poe, and Richard Scarry live?
Writer's Block

What's a quick, easy way to learn all about cliffs?
CliffsNotes

What happened when the writer got kicked out of the publisher's office?
He left with his tale tucked between his legs.

Why are authors such good people?
They always do the write thing.

Did you hear about the giant's autobiography?
It's a tall tale.

Why was Humpty Dumpty looking forward to winter?
Because he had a great fall.

When did the man finish his book on clocks?

Right on time

What is a good name for a poetry competition?

Poet Verses Poet

How do you stop someone from telling the same old stories?

Cut him off at the past.

Who was the tallest poet?

Longfellow

Who was the largest poet?

Ezra Pound

What poet is the best value?

Wordsworth

What writer had a lot of enemies?

Daniel Defoe

What writer had no money?

Edgar Allen Poe

What did Shakespeare's mother say when he and his friends got too loud?

"Keep your verses down!"

Why were A, E, I, O and U always so angry?

Irritable vowel syndrome

What do you call a young woman who is good at wordplay?

Rapunzel

What might give thee trouble?

Thy-roid.

CITY SMIRKS

What is the best place to live if you are a lawyer?

Sioux City, Iowa

What it is the best place to live if you sell football uniforms?

New Jersey

What is a good place to move if you want to gain confidence?

Boulder, Colorado

What is a good area for a pilot to live?

The Great Plains

Where shouldn't someone with high blood pressure live?

Salt Lake City, Utah

What's the best place to live if you don't like a lot of loud music?

Little Rock, Arkansas

What's the best city to learn the cost of an army headquarters?

Fort Worth, Texas

What is the best place to live if your name is Al and you're a little odd?

Albu-*quirky*, New Mexico

What's the best place to live if your name is Ann and you're a little cautious?

Cheyenne, Wyoming

MAD, MAD WORLD

Why was the section of the road near the red light so angry?
It was a crosswalk.

What does a bird do when it's angry?
It flies into a rage.

What does a rock do when it's angry?
It gets boulder.

What does an elephant do when it's angry?
It forgives but can't forget.

What do you tell an angry clown?
"Come on! Just put on a happy face."

What does a sentence do when it's angry?
It changes the subject.

What does a light bulb do when it's angry?
It's shocking.

What is the angriest pastry?
Hot cross buns

Why was the hand angry?
Its fingers were crossed.

FOOD FOR FUN

What is the worst syrup to put on pancakes?
Cough syrup

What kind of soft drink do cheerleaders like?
Root beer

What kind of sandwich saves the day?
A hero

Why did the sandwich run away?
It was a chicken sandwich.

Why didn't the students listen to the sandwich teacher?
It was a sub.

What kind of sandwich do you use to defend yourself?
   A club

What should you do if the deli doesn't have your favorite bread to make your sandwich?
   Rye-it

Where does a tomato love to take a nap?
   On a bed of lettuce

What is the most expensive roll?
   A Rolls-Royce

What is the hardest part of owning a chain restaurant?
   Finding a chef that can make chains taste good

"Do you like hot dogs?"
   "I relish them."

Why wouldn't the chef add mushrooms to the pizza?
   He didn't want to go to all that truffle.

What do you call burnt beef?
   A mis-*steak*

Why did the man yell at his dinner?
It didn't agree with him.

Why did the jar of mayonnaise lose the sword fight?
It couldn't cut the mustard.

Why did it lose the race?
It couldn't ketchup.

Where did the condiment go to recover?
The Mayo Clinic

How did the macaroni come in first?
It elbowed its way to the front.

Why did the woman always buy margarine?
She didn't know any butter.

Why did everyone love the artichoke?
Its heart was on the right plate.

Why did the dish feel ill?
It was out of sink.

What was the jar of jelly doing at the rock concert?
Jamming

Why do steaks taste better in space?

They're meteor.

Why did the hot dog quit the army?

It couldn't *mustard* the courage.

Why was the lemon afraid?

It was yellow.

What is the sweetest-tasting nut?

A dough-nut

Has the deli's food improved?

The chicken's better but the liver's wurst.

How is the deli owner's son's behavior?

The brat's wurst.

How do you cut frozen wheat?

With an ice sickle

What happened when the cake was left out in freezing temperatures?

It got frosted.

Why did the man get angry when his toaster broke?

He was lack-*toast* intolerant.

How did the restaurant pay the six-inch-tall waiter?

Under the table

Why wouldn't the man order grilled meat at the restaurant?

There was too much at steak.

Why did the woman drop out of butcher school?

She couldn't cut it.

What kind of treat is tasty, delicious, yummy, scrumptious, flavorful, appetizing, and savory?

A synonym roll

Why did the celery call the police?

It thought it was being stalked.

Why did the teddy bear not want any cake?

It was stuffed.

Why did the butter salute the popcorn?

It saw all the kernels.

Did you hear about the new restaurant they opened
on the space station?

It's got a great atmosphere and the food is
out of this world.

What kind of dessert will an octopus never eat?

Octo-pie

What kind of insect is attracted to butter?

A butterfly

Did you hear about the sick pancake?

It felt waffle.

How was the pancake's violin recital?

A little flat

What happened when the milk picked a fight?

It got creamed.

HA HA HA HA HA HA HA HA HA HA

What happened when the truck carrying strawberries overturned?

Traffic jam

What did the waiter do when the customer only tipped him four nickels?

He had a change reaction.

What kind of soup comes in a pouch?

Marsoupial

What did the mommy train engine say to the baby engine after she fed him some coal?

"Choo-choo."

LOVE LAUGHS

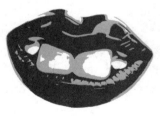

Why was the unicorn afraid to ask the girl out?

She didn't even know he existed.

Why wouldn't the man ask the woman at the bank out for a date?

He liked her but was afraid to teller.

Why did the garbage can think the man loved it?

He was always taking it out.

Why didn't the woman want to go out with the pig?

He was a boar.

Why is a horse ranch the best place to find a husband?

There are many grooms.

What did the clock say to the watch?

"I knew we would wind up together."

FAIRY FUNNY

What do you use to cook pancakes for the Lost Boys?

A Peter pan

What do you use to cook pancakes for two lost children?

A Hansel and griddle

What should you put on your door to make sure the three bears can't get in?

Goldi-locks

What are the most famous of Snow White's companions called?

Dwarf stars

How did Humpty Dumpty get over being shy?

He came out of his shell.

What do you call a discussion among the Seven Dwarfs?

Small talk

Why was the chef worried the Christmas pudding would not be ready on time?

It was the night before Christmas and not a creature was stirring.

HA HA HA

Knock, knock

Who's there?

Will

Will who?

Will you open the door, please?

Knock, knock

Who's there?

Harry

Harry who?

Close! Harry Houdini

Knock, knock

Who's there?

Echo

Echo who?

Who, who, who, who . . .

Knock, knock

Who's there?

Sue

Sue who?

I'll sue you if you don't open this door!

Knock, knock

Who's there?

Lion

Lion who?

Quit lion around and open the door.

Knock, knock
    Who's there?
Tank
    Tank who?
You're welcome!

Knock, knock
    Who's there?
Yo-de-lay-hee
    Yo-de-lay-hee
    who?
You yodel very well!

Knock, knock
    Who's there?
Butter
    Butter who?
You butter open the door!

Knock, knock
    Who's there?
Harry
    Harry who?
Harry up and open the door!

Knock, knock
    Who's there?
Who
    Who who?
Are you an owl?

Knock, knock
    Who's there?
Hi
    Hi who?
Hi-who, hi-ho, it's off to work we go!

Knock, knock
    Who's there?
Dino
    Dino who?
Dinosaur. Open the door, there's a meteorite coming!

Knock, knock
    Who's there?
Who cares? I'm tired of this joke.

About the Author

MICHAEL STRECKER is a stand-up comedian who has performed at comedy clubs throughout the United States. In addition to *Young Comic's Guide to Telling Jokes: Book 1* and *Young Comics's Guide to Telling Jokes: Book 2*, he has also published fiction for grown-ups. He lives in New Orleans with his wife and their two sons.